TH

E

G

C

Chris Martin

WAYLAND
www.waylandbooks.co.uk

First published in Great Britain in 2015 by Wayland

Copyright © Wayland 2015

Dewey Number: 005.1-dc23
ISBN: 978 0 7502 8932 0
Library ebook ISBN: 978 0 7502 8793 7

10 9 8 7 6 5 4 3 2 1

MIX
Paper from
responsible sources
FSC® C104740
FSC
www.fsc.org

Editor: Nicola Edwards
Design: Rocket Design (East Anglia) Ltd
All images and graphic elements: Shutterstock

Printed in China

Wayland
An imprint of
Hachette Children's Group
Part of Hodder & Stoughton
Carmelite House
50 Victoria Embankment
London EC4Y 0DZ

An Hachette UK Company
www.hachette.co.uk
www.hachettechildrens.co.uk

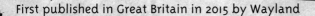

>>>CONTENTS<<<

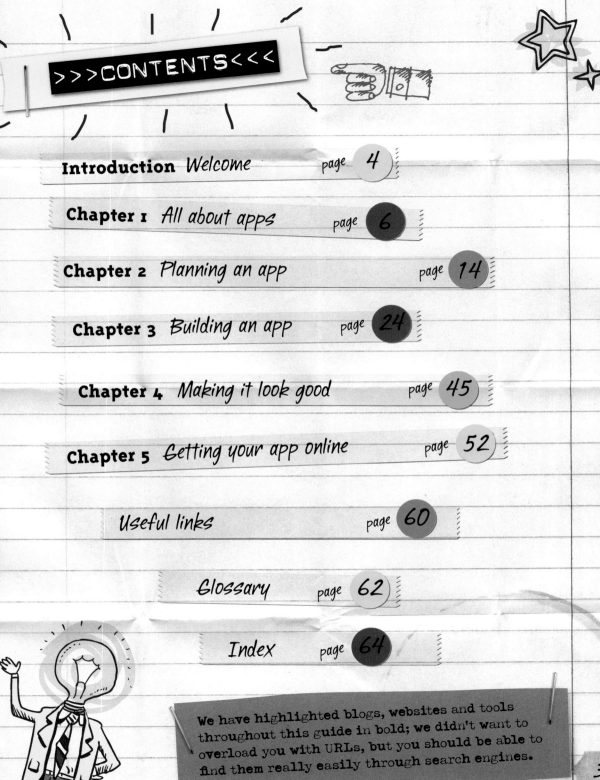

We have highlighted blogs, websites and tools throughout this guide in bold; we didn't want to overload you with URLs, but you should be able to find them really easily through search engines.

TO THE UTTERLY EXCELLENT WORLD OF APPS!

If you are lucky enough to own a smartphone, you will know that apps are where it's at. Apps turn a boring old phone from a way to call your friends and family into an all-singing, all-dancing personal computer that you can hold in your hand. Apps help us to find our way around, play games, watch video and play music. They can tell you what's on at the cinema, help you learn a language or send a message to a friend. In fact it seems that there really is an app for anything and everything.

What's great about apps is that they are quick and easy to use and because they are so simple they can be a great way to start your career as a coder or app entrepreneur.

This book will give you the inside info on apps, what they can do and how they work. We'll teach you how to get started on building your own app and making it look great. Plus we'll give you some quick expert insider tricks that mean you'll be building your app like a professional.

GET READY TO DON YOUR CODING CAP AND SUMMON YOUR CREATIVE KARMA FOR THE QUICK EXPERT TEAM'S SHOW-AND-TELL ON:

The teenage app-builder who **made millions**

How to be an app **entrepreneur**

How to **write code** and create your own app

How to speak app: **learn the lingo** from 4G to GPS

The **low-down** on the tricks the professionals use to build apps

Chapter 1

ALL ABOUT APPS

✳ WHAT IS AN APP?

Apps are amazing! They are changing our world by making access to powerful computing available wherever and whenever we want it. 'App' is simply an abbreviation of the word *application* and is the name for a powerful piece of software that can run independently on a smartphone, PC or other electronic device. Usually an app will perform a specific task (like telling you the weather) and can be downloaded for a small cost or even for free.

When most people talk about apps, they mean the little, self contained programs used to add functionality to a mobile device like an **Android phone, iPhone, BlackBerry** or a tablet device like an **iPad**. An example would be Snapchat, an app that allows you to send a picture (for a few seconds!) to a friend.

There are also **desktop apps** or online apps that you can access to complete specific tasks while online instead of the heavier software (such as Microsoft Word) that lives permanently on your computer.

✳ APPS BASICS — DESKTOP VS MOBILE APPS

So the word 'app' can mean a few different things. Let's have a closer look at two of the most common types of app:

Desktop apps are gateways to online services and can be used to run software on your PC. Traditionally if you wanted to use a program you would have to buy it on a disc or download an installation file and then install it. A desktop app will quickly let you use the same functionality through an interface that uses software hosted on the Internet. Think

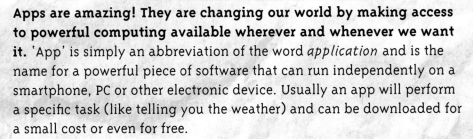

of it like installing your own librarian who can give you just the books you want rather than installing a whole library. These desktops apps are usually offered as 'Software as a Service' (SAAS) where you have to sign up for an account — typically paying a monthly or one-off fee.

Mobile apps are used to extend the functionality of a mobile device — usually a smartphone — beyond just making calls, sending texts and checking emails. Mobile apps might be games or groovy gadgets to tell you the weather or find your nearest bus stop. Like desktop apps some mobile apps need to access the Internet to work but many do not. You may have to pay a small price to download a mobile app but hundreds of thousands of them are free or only require you to pay for extra functionality.

For the purpose of this book when we talk about apps we are talking about mobile apps... so before we get started on building one we need to examine what they can do.

✳ WHAT CAN APPS DO?

We've seen that a mobile app is a piece of software that runs on a smartphone to complete a specific task. However what makes apps really special is that they can use the features of a smartphone they live on to do incredible things.

There are four key elements of smartphone functionality used by apps:

Knowing where you are: Apps can use the Global Positioning System (GPS) in a smartphone to find out where you are, find what's nearby (such as shops, cinemas or even your friends) and to get directions to those places.

Buying stuff: An app can use your contract with your smartphone's service provider or an **iTunes** or **Paypal** account to let you buy things with your phone. This means you can order goods online, buy and download In App content or access subscription-based services.

Internal sensors: Your smartphone has an internal **gyroscope** and an **accelerometer** so it knows where it is in space (and so where you are). This means you can perform a task simply by moving the handset. For example, the layout of a page can change from landscape to portrait depending on whether the phone is being held upright or on its side.

>> THE BOFFIN BIT <<

iOS

iOS (or Internet Operating System) was developed by Apple inc and is what makes Apple's mobile devices like the iPhone, iPad or iPod run all the stuff you want them to do. It was introduced in 2007 was originally known as iPhone OS.

Adjusting settings in iOS allows you to change the appearance of your device (such as the brightness of the screen), to change how the device works (e.g. adding a pass code to lock the screen) or to complete networking tasks (such as connecting to Wi-Fi). iOS also runs any apps you might install.

iOS is specially designed for mobile devices, so it is smaller, faster and uses less power. Its touch interface means you can use your fingers to control programs rather than needing a mouse.

Soon after the launch of iOS, Apple released an SDK (Software Development Kit) that allowed developers to build their own apps for iOS. Apple also releases its own changes and updates to the iOS annually.

Touchscreen: You can input data into a smartphone in lots of different ways through its touchscreen. Apps on your smartphone can allow you to manipulate content with your fingers, so you can zoom in or draw pictures, play games, or do pretty much whatever you want....

It is worth having a think about how useful these functions are. When and where might you need to buy something with your smartphone, for example? Consider too how smartphone functionality has been used by other app builders. For example, how does a game of Angry Birds use a touchscreen or a social networking app like Facebook use messaging? Examining how others have used these features will help you to develop ideas about how you could use them in your own app.

✳ A BRIEF HISTORY OF MOBILE PHONES

An app isn't going to be much use without a smartphone. These days so many people have smartphones that it is difficult to imagine a world without them, but mobile phones have only been around for the last 15 years. Here's a brief history of their development.

The first mobile phone

The story of the modern mobile phones began in the 1940s when engineers working at AT&T in America developed powerful electric cells to boost the output of base stations that transmitted radio signals. This allowed one base station to cover a wide area. These super stations powered early mobile communication between vehicles that needed to keep in touch like ambulances, police cars and taxis. While these early devices are often referred to as 0G, or Zero Generation, mobile phones, in reality they were more like two-way radios.

>> THE BOFFIN BIT <<

WI-FI

Wi-Fi is the name given to the clever technology that allows electronic devices to send and receive high volumes of data or connect to the Internet using radio waves rather than a physical connection through a wire.

As well as smartphones, many devices use Wi-Fi, for example PCs, video-game consoles and tablets. These can all connect to a network resource (like the Internet) via a Wireless Network Access Point (commonly known as a Wi-Fi hotspot).

By connecting to a network rather than having small chunks of data broadcast to your device, you are able to complete tasks that require a lot of bandwidth such as streaming video or playing online games.

The name Wi-Fi is a play on words from the term Hi-Fi (or high fidelity) used to describe top end audio equipment (so technically Wi-Fi means Wireless Fidelity). Wi-Fi is maintained by a trade association known as the Wi-Fi Alliance. This association is responsible for ensuring that any device offering or using Wi-Fi technology is up to standard and secure.

The development of mobile phone technology

The Americans took the next step forward in mobile telephony when a Motorola employee called Martin Cooper invented the first mobile phone that was fit for general use. Cooper made communications history in April 1973 when he made a call to a press conference in New York on the prototype of a hand-held mobile phone.

But it was not until the mid-1980s that First Generation (1G) networks were launched. These included handover technology that meant users didn't lose connections between base stations so that conversations would not be interrupted. The Motorola Dynatac 8000 (known as the 'brick' due to its chunky battery) was one of the first commercially available mobile phones to use the new technology. It went on sale in 1983 priced at an eye-watering $4000 — about £3000.

Affordable mobile phones

The birth of the Second Generation (2G) mobile phones was in Finland in 1993. It was also the year that the first text messages (SMS or Short Message Service) were sent and that data services began to appear on mobile phones. With it came a host of smaller 'candy bar' style handsets from Scandinavian operators such as Nokia and Ericsson that were lighter and cheaper to buy.

In 2002 Nokia and Ericsson pushed forward again with their T39 and 3510i models. These introduced Bluetooth for fast data connection and the first mobile Internet connection to a phone.

Smartphone revolution

While mobile phones continued to get more sophisticated, it was not until 2007 that the first successful smartphone was introduced, Apple's iPhone was an instant success. It combined email, phone calling and music in one device and revolutionized both the design of mobile phones and how people used them.

Today's mobiles

The mobile phones that most of us use today are 3G, or Third Generation devices. 3G launched in 2009. Large amounts of data could be transferred to mobile phones with 3G and as handsets were more powerful, operators could offer a range of services that used the Internet to support installed apps. 4G promises even faster data delivery. This means how we use our smartphones will change once again as we become more connected than ever before.

✳ MOBILE PLATFORMS

Now it starts to get tricky, because with lots of different companies building smartphones for the different networks that were used for calls and data, the market was quickly flooded with different products that worked in different ways.

As a result not all smartphones look the same, work the same or even use the same **Operating System** (or mobile OS). We will have to bear this in mind when designing our app. When building an app the operating system is very important as it is the underlying code that runs the device and any apps that run on top of it. Another way of thinking about how apps work with an operating system is to imagine that your smartphone is a house. The operating system provides the doors, windows, water and electricity while apps are the furniture inside it.

There are many different operating systems but the three main ones are Apple's **iOS** found in its iPhones and iPads, **Google's Android OS** used by companies such as Samsung and Nokia and the **Blackberry OS** used by that company's handsets and tablets.

Even trickier, each operating system is built using a different programming language, such as Java, Objective C, and C++ to name but a few. These languages are extremely powerful and can tap into the source code of a phone's operating system to access internal functionality and controls. Apps built in this way are called **native apps**.

These programming languages are amazing, but they take a long time to learn. That's no good for a Quick Expert. This is why we will be creating what's known as a **hybrid app**. This is an app that combines the power of the Internet with the convenience of an app by using an easy-to-access language called **HTML 5**. While we won't be able to use as much of the functionality of the phone, we will be able to produce a good looking app that works on any operating system.

THE ANDROID STORY

When Google became, well, Google, they made so much money that they began buying lots of smaller 'start-up' companies that might have good ideas that they could use to improve their service. One such company was Android Inc which specialized in developing smart mobile devices. Two year later on the 5th of November 2007 Google launched its own operating system called (surprise, surprise) Android.

The question everyone asked was why Google bothered to make an operating system when there were loads of other systems available. One reason was that Google Android was an opensource system and that meant anybody could use the code. The second was that it was modular – a bit like Lego – so developers could share packages of code to connect together things like GPS functionality, maps and web information.

Both these things meant more people could get mobile and still use Google's products. Despite being primarily designed for phones, it also has been used in tablets, televisions and even cameras.

QUICK EXPERT SUMMARY

- There are desktop and mobile apps.

- There are four key elements of smartphone technology used by apps – GPS, commerce functionality, touchscreens and internal sensors.

- The first mobile phone call was made in 1973.

- Modern smartphones use 3G and 4G technology.

- Different smartphones use different operating systems.

PLANNING AN APP

* WHY PLAN?

So it looks like apps are pretty cool. But before we jump in and try to build one of our own we need to plan how it will work. We need to plan because for an app to work well it has to take into account what environment it will live in (remember all those different handsets and operating systems) and how people might use it.

Modern smartphones and tablets are amazing and they contain a huge amount of processing power but they are different to a desktop or laptop computer in two crucial ways — the screen size available to them (it's smaller) and the way people are likely to input data (with their fingers rather than a mouse). This means that for any app to be easy to use it will need to be simple to understand and easy to control as people won't have a huge screen and a mouse to help them.

Apps are all about getting what you want quickly, whether it is reaching the next level of your favourite game or finding out what is on TV tonight. Any content you publish will need to be short and concise — if you want to write an essay you can do that at school.

As a result of these factors, function and design are crucial when thinking about how any app will work. It sounds scary but luckily there are a few easy techniques that can help us do this without writing a line of code.

REALITY CHECK

 Nick D'Aloisio

Nick D'Aloisio taught himself to code at the age of 12 and was just 15 when he created an app called Summly while revising for his mock GCSEs in 2011. Nick started with the belief that as we live in a world of constant information, it would be great to find a new way to simplify how we found the stories that were important to us. His app condensed news articles into three key paragraphs that could fit onto an iPhone screen. Users could also customize the news categories and link to the original article if they liked the summary.

When Nick was 17, he sold the app to Internet search giant Yahoo! for $30million. Nick also started a full-time job with the web giant helping to integrate his new technology into their products. All while studying for his A-levels!

Despite becoming a teenage millionaire, Nick carried on living with his family in Wimbledon and said he had 'boring' plans for the money.

"I'm planning to invest it – my parents are in control of it," he said. "But I want to buy a shoulder bag."

OFFICIAL FORM C-185/A

✳ WHAT WILL YOUR APP DO?

An app is fundamentally a tool that helps people to do things (such as choose a train journey from a timetable). It's different from something like a website that is a device for publishing content (as a magazine does). This means that a good app is designed to take people on a simple, straightforward journey to help them achieve what they want with the least effort.

Creating a question

To work out how your app will work as a tool, ask yourself the question 'What will my app do?' The best way to help you focus is to write down the answer, for example: I want my app to help people choose the best pet for them.

Finding the answer

When you know what your app will do (in our example help people choose a pet) it's time to work out how the app will do it. This is a four-step process:

Step 1: Your app will need to know some information about the person using it to recommend a pet. Think about the factors that would be most important to people when choosing a pet. This might be cost, where people live or if they have any allergies. Then think about what potential questions people might need to answer to give you that information. For example: Do they have a garden? Are they allergic to fur? How much do they want to spend? Finally you might like to throw in a fun factor like cuteness. Do they like cuddly or scary animals?

Step 2: If each of these questions were on a single page, think about the answers to these questions. The answers to 'Where do you live?' might be 'In a small flat', 'In a house with a patio' or 'In a house with a garden', whereas the answers to 'How much do you want to spend?' might be '£5', '£10', '£15' or 'over £20'.

Now you know where people will start (wanting to choose a pet) and what they will have to do along the way (tell you about themselves) it's time to think about the end point to their journey through your app.

Step 3: Think about the different ways in which people might end their journey and leave the app with the information they need. In this case, it will be about types of pet, such as a gerbil, cat, dog or snake. You could include a picture and some basic information about each pet.

Step 4: Now we're getting somewhere because when you match your end point to the information you have collected, you will have an idea of how people will get to it. You will probably find that people could get to the same place in a number of different ways. For example a gerbil will suit people who live in a flat, are not allergic to fur, like cuddly animals and want to spend about £5.

>> THE BOFFIN BIT <<

4G

4G is the fourth generation of mobile phone technology. 2G technology was suitable for making calls and sending text messages while 3G made it possible to access the internet and receive emails more effectively through your mobile phone. But what's so great about 4G?

4G services should make it much quicker to surf the web on your mobile, tablet or laptop by offering data delivery speeds that are nearer to what you currently experience with home broadband.

Because of this, 4G will be ideally for video streaming, mapping and 'always on' services like social networking sites. For the typical user, download speeds of initial 4G networks could be around 5-7 times faster than those for existing 3G networks. This means that a whole album of music that takes 20 minutes to download on a 3G phone will take just 3 minutes on 4G. Wowzah!

✳ PLANNING A USER JOURNEY

Now it is time to bring all of this together so you have a plan from which to build your app. The easiest way to do this is to create a map of how the people accessing your app will use it. This is a called a user journey map. These are pretty simple to create and will be an invaluable way to get a good sense of how your app will work.

Start with a large piece of A3 paper. At the top draw a box. This will represent the first page of your app — the home screen that will carry the title of your app and tell people what it does. Label it **Home screen**.

Then draw another box underneath it. This will represent the next page users will go to — in this case to answer the first question you ask them about themselves. As this page asks questions rather than gives information you might like to draw it as a different shape — like a large diamond. Label this **About you**. Then draw a diamond for each of the questions in a line underneath. Label each of these appropriately, e.g. **About your allergies** or **About your house**. Finally create pages for each of your pet choices. Remember these do not ask questions but give information, so draw the boxes as rectangles like the Home Screen. Label these with the types of pet e.g. **Gerbil** or **Snake**.

To complete your user journey map, draw arrows that indicate where people using your app will go. In some cases people might go back and forth between pages. In this case draw a line that has arrows at both ends.

When you are finished, your user journey map should look like the diagram at the top of page 19.

Each of the boxes you have drawn represents a page you will need to build in your app and a stage people will need to move through as they use it. Now it's time to plan how these pages will look.

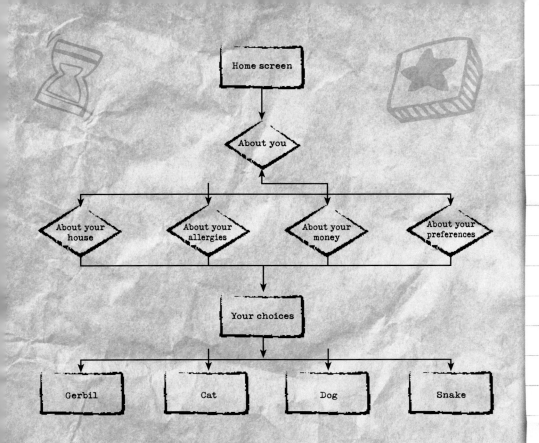

✳ PAPER PROTOTYPING

We could have the best user journey map in the world but if people don't know which button to press or link to follow the app won't work. So it's equally important to think about how each page will look and paper prototyping is a great way to do this.

Paper prototyping is simply drawing the elements that make up your app, such as buttons, pictures, text boxes and headings, on paper and then laying them out on a second sheet of paper that represents the screen your user will interact with.

It sounds simple and it is. This technique is used by professional app designers to test their designs with real people before they put a lot of effort into coding. It is part of a practice known as user testing. The best thing about it is that if you want to change something you just move a bit of paper, draw something else or throw it away and start again.

So what do you do?

- ◉ Take a large piece of paper and draw a rectangle on it to represent your 'screen'.

- ◉ Draw the elements you want to represent to scale on a separate piece of paper. Be sure to label them, for example 'Button' or draw what it is if it's an image or some squiggles for a piece of text.

- ◉ Draw a line around each element and then cut around the outside of the line with scissors.

- ◉ Lay out the elements on your paper 'screen'.

Voila! Instant app.

Once you have created your app in paper form, get a friend or family member to take a look at it and ask them to complete a few tasks. Where would they click to get to the next page, where would they find information about the app or even how would they get in touch with the developer? Get them to point at the prototype and talk out loud so you know what they're thinking.

Remember, everyone does things in different ways, so there is no right or wrong answer. Usability is the study of feedback on the design of apps and websites and it can teach you a lot. You can use people's ideas to make your app better.

And of course, if you need to create a new element simply draw it and add it in.

>> THE BOFFIN BIT <<

USABILITY

We all use apps differently. Usability is the name given to the study of how easy it is to read, use or navigate an app. You need to think about usability when you design your pages, as you want your users to spend more time viewing your content than trying to work out where everything is.

Here are a couple of key tips for usability that you should try to follow:

- ◉ Keep your app simple.

- ◉ Ensure each page loads fast.

- ◉ Try to fit content onto a single screen so there is no scrolling.

- ◉ Lay out each page to make it easy for users to find things quickly.

- ◉ Ensure your links or buttons are easy and obvious.

✳ BADGING YOUR APP

The app you create will be competing with hundreds of thousands of others on the **App Store** or **Play Store**, so you will need to badge it to make it stand out. Think of a catchy name for your app that sounds fun but which also describes what it does. Something like **Pet Finder** or **Pet Guru** — though you can probably come up with something much better.

Have a go at creating an engaging image that you can put on the home screen and use to brand your app — for example, a dog with a magnifying glass. You can use the same image to make an icon for the app. This will this make your app a bit more fun and help to make it easily recognizable. One quick tip — the App and Play Stores will always display your icon next to text so avoid using text in your icon to help it stand out.

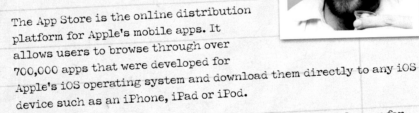

>> THE BOFFIN BIT <<

THE APP STORE

The App Store is the online distribution platform for Apple's mobile apps. It allows users to browse through over 700,000 apps that were developed for Apple's iOS operating system and download them directly to any iOS device such as an iPhone, iPad or iPod.

The apps found in the App Store may be downloaded for free or for a small fee. When an app is bought Apple takes 30 per cent of the price with the remaining 70 per cent going to the app's publisher.

As all the apps displayed on the App Store are designed specifically for iOS, Apple check items by independent developers for quality before they make them available for download.

The App Store can be accessed directly on the Internet or via an installed app. Since its launch in 2008, over 400 million accounts have been created and some 40 billion apps downloaded.

SAY WHAT?

> So, three things: a widescreen iPod with touch controls; a revolutionary mobile phone; and a breakthrough Internet communications device. An iPod, a phone, and an Internet communicator. An iPod, a phone ... are you getting it? These are not three separate devices.

Steve Jobs, founder of Apple invents the smartphone

QUICK EXPERT SUMMARY

- Ensure your app is useful and functional.
- Before your start, think carefully about what your app will do.
- Plan your app's user journey so that it is easy to use.
- Use paper prototyping to plan the layout of your app.
- Badge your app with an engaging image.

BUILDING AN APP

✳ GETTING STARTED

There are three key steps to building an app quickly and easily with HTML 5. The first is making a website, which will mean learning the basics of coding in HTML 5 and some CSS (Cascading Style Sheets) for design. The second is uploading your code to a piece of software that will package it up so that it runs as an app on Android or iOS phones. Finally you load the results into the App Store and Play Store for people to download to their smartphones.

Don't worry, it is easier that it sounds. Most of this will be free and we will take you through each step in this book. But you will need to start with the fun bit — learning a bit of code. Sound good? Then grab your coding goggles and let's get on with it.

(There's no such thing as coding goggles. We just like to pretend there is.)

✳ WHAT IS HTML 5?

HTML 5 is the fifth version of the markup language used to build web pages and present content on them. It was designed by the W3C (the World Wide Web Consortium, the people who set the standards for the Internet) so the same code could be used on a wide range of browsers. Having one standard also meant that web pages could be used on PCs, laptops, smartphones or even digital TVs.

W3C also wanted to simplify commonly used tags and change the language to fit with how people wanted to use it; for example by coming up with a way to add popular multimedia (such as video and audio) without needing an additional program to play it.

Just like earlier versions of HTML, HTML 5 is designed to be free and simple to use. It works by wrapping tags around pieces of content (text, links or images) to create code that will tell a browser how you'd like your page laid out. Learn the tags and a few basics and you're away!

>> THE BOFFIN BIT <<

HTML

HTML is the authoring language used to create web pages on the Internet. It was invented in 1990 by a scientist called Tim Berners-Lee. His purpose was to make it easier for scientists at different universities to see to each other's work. However by inventing HTML and creating the principle of sharing information across computer networks he laid the foundation for today's World Wide Web.

HTML is short for HyperText Markup Language. Hyper is the opposite of linear and means you can go wherever you want with it; Text is well, text; Markup is what you do to the text (e.g. adding headings and bullets) and Language is what HTML is because it uses many English words.

The information HTML gives a browser is the information it needs to display the structure and layout of a web page. It does this by wrapping content in a variety of tags and attributes. Tags are also used to specify hypertext links that allow users to jump to other pages by clicking on an image, button or sentence.

✳ HOW DO YOU WRITE HTML 5?

The good news is that HTML 5 is easy to learn because it follows some fairly simple rules. All you will need is an eye for detail, a computer and a bit of practice.

If you know a bit of HTML already you won't discover too many surprises in HTML 5 because it is built around a library of **tags** used in earlier versions of the language. To distinguish HTML tags from normal text, these tags are always framed by angle brackets <and>. You'll find these brackets on your keyboard just above the comma and the full stop (on the same buttons as them).

The written instructions to the browser found between these brackets are called **elements**. While these elements look like some kind of complex code, in fact they are usually basic abbreviations of the tag's purpose and pretty easy to work out.

For example, the tag **<img>** tells your browser that you are adding an image.

A tag may also have **attributes** within it. This is additional information about how to use the tag.

For example, **height=45** tells the browser to display your image 45 pixels high.

Types of HTML tag

Like any language, HTML is constantly changing and growing as it evolves. For a start, there are two kinds of HTML tag: **container tags** and **empty tags**.

A container tag wraps around **copy** (text or graphics) and comes in a set that has a matching opening and closing tag. For example:

<html> is an opening tag.
</html> is a closing tag.

Everything after the opening tag will be affected by the element while the forward slash (/) in the closing tag tells the browser that the instruction has ended.

However empty tags stand on their own. For example the tag <br> or break (told you they were easy to work out) tells the browser to add a line break. Empty tags do not have to be wrapped around copy and do not require a closing.

The good news is that there is only a handful of empty tags and — to be fair — it's not a problem with HTML 5's newer tags, so as a general rule assume that every tag you open will need to be closed.

>> THE BOFFIN BIT <<

HACK

Hack is a much used word in computing that has a range of meanings from illegally breaking into a computer network to modifying the software on your own computer. Increasingly 'hacking' refers to the process of working in groups to create new software products or apps. This process is marked by how quickly the products are created (often in a single day) and the fact that the process is open to anyone to take part in.

A Hack Day is an event where computer programmers come together to build a prototype for a piece of software. Hack Days tend to be a lot of fun and are marked by a friendly spirit of competition (and the consumption of a lot of pizza).

Ideas, processes, user flows and designs can all be hacked. Holding a Hack Day can be a great way to bring your friends together to help you make your app even better.

※ MAKING A PAGE IN HTML 5

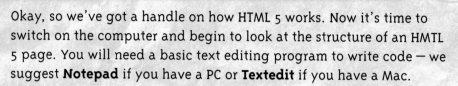

Okay, so we've got a handle on how HTML 5 works. Now it's time to switch on the computer and begin to look at the structure of an HMTL 5 page. You will need a basic text editing program to write code — we suggest **Notepad** if you have a PC or **Textedit** if you have a Mac.

All HTML 5 pages are divided into two main parts: the **head** and the **body**. The head contains information about the page and the body holds the content that will be displayed.

So far, so good. To create your first page you will need four primary tags: <html>, <head>, <title> and <body>. These are all container tags, so remember that they must have a beginning and an end.

<html> </html>

Every HTML page begins and ends with the <html> tag. This tells the browser that the document is an HTML file.

<head> </head>

The <head> tag contains general information about the page, such as keywords for search engines or a description.

<title> </title>

The <title> tag appears within the <head> tag and tells the browser the title of the page, for example 'Pet Guru'.

<body> </body>

The main content of your page is placed within the body tags, for example text, pictures, buttons and links.

So a simple HMTL page would look like this:

```
<html>
<head>
<title Pet Guru /title>
</head>
<body>
```

Welcome to Pet Guru

```
</body>
</html>
```

It really is that simple.

You don't have to space your tags out as we have done (because a computer won't care) but it helps to do so when writing code as it will make it easier to read.

REALITY CHECK

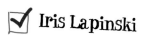 ☑ Iris Lapinski

Iris Lapinski is the CEO of the UK-based Apps for Good, a nonprofit organization that teaches teenagers to create apps that solve problems they care about and help to change their world. She thinks that if you only ask 35-year-old male developers what apps they can come up with, you won't see much that is truly innovative. However if you ask people who have a different perspective on life and different experiences, 14-year-old girls for example, they will come up with some really interesting ideas for apps.

Apps for Good was founded in 2009. The programme has been delivered in over 100 schools and has introduced basic app making skills to more than 5,000 11-18-year-olds across the U.K. *The Observer* newspaper named Lapinski as one of Britain's '50 New Radicals' for her work with Apps for Good. She says: "What we're trying to do is to democratize app development."

* WHAT ARE SEMANTIC ELEMENTS?

One of the key differences that HTML 5 has from earlier versions of HTML is its use of semantic elements. These are tags that explain the purpose of a section of code to a browser (or another coder). For example, which part of the page is the top of the document (or header).

Below are a few of the semantic elements found in HTML 5:

`<article>`

`<footer>`

`<header>`

`<nav>`

`<section>`

Because these semantic elements are meant to be descriptive for coders as well as machines, you can probably guess what most of them do.

Stuck? Well, if you must know...

Header tells the browser about information at the top of the page.

Nav shows where the menu bar is to help people navigate. **Section** and **Article** can be used to show that your content is broken into useable bunches.

Finally, **Footer** contains additional things you might want to keep at the bottom of the page like contact information.

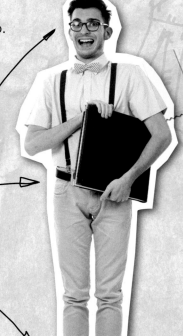

Essentially you can use them like this:

```
┌─────────────────────────────────────────┐
│                                         │
│               Header                    │
│                                         │
├─────────────────────────────────────────┤
│                                         │
│                Nav                      │
│                                         │
├─────────────────────────────────────────┤
│              Section                    │
│                                         │
│  ┌───────────────────────────────────┐  │
│  │            Article                │  │
│  └───────────────────────────────────┘  │
│  ┌───────────────────────────────────┐  │
│  │            Article                │  │
│  └───────────────────────────────────┘  │
│                                         │
├─────────────────────────────────────────┤
│                                         │
│               Footer                    │
│                                         │
└─────────────────────────────────────────┘
```

And you can do it in the code by doing this:

```
<html>

<head>

<title>Pet Guru</title>

</head>

<body>

<header>Hello and welcome to Pet Guru.</header>

<section>An application that helps you choose a pet that suits you.

<article>Cute pets</article>
```

```
<article>Scary pets</article>

<article>Hairy pets</article>

</section>

<footer>Contact me</footer>

</body>

</html>
```

Does the laying out of elements like this seem familiar after Chapter 2? That's right, while the positioning of these elements will be set using a CSS styling (see more about this in chapter 4), the descriptiveness of the HTML makes it super easy for you to tell the browser how to lay out your page exactly like your paper prototype.

Nesting

As the number of tags on your page grows you will need to find a way to navigate them. The best way to do this is to structure your web page using nesting. This means that each new set of tags is placed inside other tags like the layers of an onion.

On our page the <title> tags are nested inside the <head> tags, while <head> and <body> tags are nested inside the <html> tags. Remember that you will have to close all the container tags that you have opened so nesting is good way to keep track of them.

Okay, it's the moment of truth. Let's create and save your first HTML 5 document.

DIY DUDE

Working with HTML 5

Open your text editor and write in the code laid out on pages 31 and 32. If you are using TextEdit on a Mac, make sure you have switched to plain text format under the Format menu.

When you have finished, open the File menu and using the 'Save as' function save your file to somewhere easy to find... like your desktop. You can name the file whatever you like but professional developers usually go for "index". It is very important that you add ".html" to the end so the browser knows that it is a HTML 5 page, for example "index.html".

To view your page, open your browser – any browser such as Internet Explorer, Safari or Google Chrome will do – go to the browser's File menu, select 'Open file' and navigate to your page.

There it is! You've made your first page!

✳ FORMATTING TEXT

So now you have your first HTML 5 page. Some of you quicker experts may have noticed that to add text to your page you simply type whatever you like between the <body> tags. But hold your horses because you can use other tags to make this text easier to read and a lot more interesting to look at.

Titles and headings

You can create titles in your page by using the **heading tag**. This is represented in HTML 5 as (you guessed it) <h>. There are six levels of heading tag ranging from <h1> to <h6>. These tags will change the size of your text from BIG <h1> to small <h6>.

Behind the scenes, heading tags also serve a vital purpose by telling browsers what the most important information on your page is based on the heading tags you have used. So it is important that your tags run in order with the most important thing first. For example, the title:

`<h1>Hello and welcome to the Pet Guru app</h1>`

Spacing and formatting

To create paragraphs and add space between them you use the paragraph tag. No prizes for guessing that this is represented in HTML 5 as `<p>`. This is a container tag and wraps around the text that makes up each individual paragraph.

For example:

`<p> An application that helps you choose a pet that suits you.</p>`

To add a single line of space, you can use the break tag represented as `<br>`. As we saw earlier in the book, this is an empty tag and stands alone so you won't need to wrap it.

For example:

`Cute pets<br>`

`Scary pets<br>`

`Hairy pets`

Adding emphasis to words and phrases

You may also want to add emphasis to words in the text using bold or italics. To create bold text use: `<strong>...</strong>` and for italicized text use: `<i>...</i>`. Using `<mark>...</mark>` will highlight a section.

It is worth noting that while most browsers will render these tags, HTML 5 sees them as more of a description of the text (our old friend semantic markup) than a tag, so you may be better to render these effects in CSS (see page 45).

>> THE BOFFIN BIT <<

TABLETS

A tablet, or tablet computer, is a small computer that combines its data input, display and battery functions in a single, mobile unit. Probably the most famous example of a tablet is Apple's iPad.

While tablets can do most things a PC can do, they also have many of the features of mobile phones like cameras, gyroscopes and accelerometers, making them great for communicating on the move. While some tablets have a few buttons most are controlled by a touchscreen and virtual keyboard rather than a keyboard and a mouse.

Tablets are typically larger than smartphones but they are effectively the same, except that they have traded the ability to make telephone calls for a larger screen and more processing power. It's no surprise that tablets use apps a lot and they also come in a variety of sizes from mini tablets to hybrid designs that are as large as a PC screen.

✳ ADDING LISTS

You may have a lot to say but you need to be careful that your page will be easy to read on a small screen. Big blocks of dense text will make it hard going for readers, so an easy way to present content that falls together under a single topic is in a list. Lists in HMTL 5 can be presented as both numbered or **ordered lists**, and bulleted or **unordered lists**.

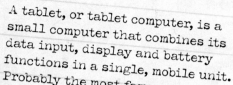

Lists are nested. This means that there is a pair of nested tags that identify the type of list and then within that tag there are other tags that itemize each element or **list item**. For example:

`<ol>...</ol>`
The ordered list is a container tag and is used for numbered lists.

`<ul>...</ul>`
The unordered list is a container tag and is used for bulleted lists.

`<li>...</li>`
The list item tag is a container tag and is nested within the ordered or unordered tags.

You can see the difference between the two list styles below.

An **ordered (numbered) list** is coded like this:

```
<ol>
<li>Cute pets</li>
<li>Scary pets </li>
<li>Hairy pets </li>
</ol>
```

In the browser it will look like this:

1. Cute pets
2. Scary pets
3. Hairy pets

An **unordered (bulleted) list** is coded like this:

```
<ul>
<li>Cute pets</li>
<li>Scary pets</li>
<li>Hairy pets</li>
</ul>
```

In the browser it will look like this:

• Cute pets
• Scary pets
• Hairy pets

It's now time to update your HTML pages using some of the new code we've learned. You might also start adding your own content. You could use the text we've suggested while you were learning or start adding your own if you want to start building your app straight away.

DIY DUDE
Update your HTML 5 page

Open up your HTML file in your editing program and type in the additional text (or your own text) and code that we've looked at. Don't forget to try the paragraph and list tags. When you've finished, save the page by using the 'Save' function in the File menu. Or get fancy by saving with a keyboard shortcut by hitting the S key while holding down the CTRL button. Use the Apple button instead of CTRL if you've got a Mac.

Now return to your browser. Nothing has happened, right?

Don't panic, all you need to do is refresh the page to see the changes you have made. You can find the 'Refresh' or 'Reload' option under the View menu. Alternately use a keyboard shortcut again, in this case by hitting the 'F5' key on your keyboard while holding down the CTRL or Apple buttons. Your changes should now appear.

By amending your HTML 5 file and refreshing the browser as you go, you will be able to browse the changes as you make them and slowly build up your page.

✳ ADDING IMAGES AND VIDEO

Words on a page are pretty good, but you'll need pictures and video to really make your app come alive. Whether it is a photograph, YouTube video or a cartoon, remember they should add something to your content so use them to illustrate what you are saying in words.

It's easy to browse and download your choice of images from the millions available online. Simply go to the Google website and click the Images tab at the top of the page. Now you can browse images from all over the Internet. If you find one you like, simply right click and hit 'Save picture as' to download it to your computer.

Video is even easier to access if you use a site like YouTube. Simply click the 'Share' button beneath your favourite video and YouTube will show you the URL link for that video. You can cut and paste this into your code to display the video on your website.

Copyright of images and video

Before you go picture-mad you should be aware of copyright law. While it is easy to find pictures and videos online, technically, using other people's images could be an infringement of copyright law.

In practice, you're allowed 'fair use' of images, which means that if you properly credit the owner and only use them on a personal website, there shouldn't be a problem.

A good way around this issue is to play it safe and use images that have already been cleared for use by everyone. When looking at Google Images, click 'Search tools' and then 'Labeled for reuse' to find copyright free images. There are also banks of images, such as on the website Morguefile, most of which are copyright free. You can also search using the Creative Commons website which draws on various image banks. You will usually need to give a credit somewhere if you use a picture that you've found on one of these websites; you can find more details on their Help pages.

Image and video formats

Both images and video can use a lot of computer memory so big images will make your page load slowly. You will need to be particularly aware of this when building your app because if people are using a slower data connection it will take them longer to download it. They may be using their data allowances to pay for the privilege, too. In short, no one will thank you for big images in an app.

If you want to make really professional looking images you will need some graphics software. You can also use this to reduce the size of any images or photographs you use. You might like to look at

Adode Photoshop or Paintshop Pro (a shareware program), but a free opensource alternative is the GNU Image Manipulation Program which can be downloaded at www.gimp.org.

Special file formats for images are commonly used to reduce the amount of memory they will use. These are GIF (Graphic Interchange Format) files that are good for simple images such as logos; JPEG (Joint Photographic Experts Group) files that are good for photographs; and PNG (Portable Network Graphic) files (pronounced ping) that are pretty good at everything and will probably give you the smallest image size.

✳ THE IMAGE TAG

To place an image onto your page you will need to use the **image tag `<img>`**. There are two very important things to remember about the image tag. It's an empty tag so there's no closing tag but it will require **attributes** to be effective. If you remember, an attribute is the word coders used to describe extra data for the browser about a tag's function for example the size of the image.

The code for adding an image tag looks like this:

src – identifies the image's name and tells the browser where to get it

height and width – tells the browser the size of the image in pixels

```
<img src="files/petguru_logo.jpg" width="149"
height="140" alt="Picture of Pet Guru logo">
```

alt – gives alternative text to describe the image. This is read by search engines such as Google and used by assistive software such as screen readers used by blind people

>> THE BOFFIN BIT <<

GPS

GPS or the Global Positioning System is how your phone or tablet knows where you are and can serve you location-based information. Incredible though it seems, GPS accesses a network of satellites orbiting the Earth and location information can be provided in all weather conditions, anywhere on the planet where there is an unobstructed line of sight to four or more GPS satellites.

The system was developed in 1973 and is maintained by the United States government; though it is mainly used by the military and the civil government, it is also freely accessible to anyone around the world who has a GPS receiver (such as a smartphone).

Perhaps you are wondering how your phone still knows where you are even if you are inside a building. Some applications (such as Google Maps) will also triangulate your position using information from the radio masts or Wi-Fi hotspots accessed by your phone. Scary stuff you may think, but the ability to work out where you need to go or the location of your nearest cinema at the touch of button makes GPS pretty useful.

✳ THE VIDEO TAG

Adding a video to your page is very similar process but you will need to use the video tag 'video'. Unlike the image tag, the video tag is a container tag and it will require both attributes and an additional empty tag called 'source' for it to work.

The code for adding a video tag looks like this:

```
<video width="320" height="240" controls autoplay>
<source src= petmovie.mp4" type="video/mp4">
Your browser does not support the video tag.
</video>
```

The video tag attributes are:

Height & width tells the browser the size of the image in pixels.

Controls tells the browser how to play a video

The source tag attributes are:

src identifies the video's name and tells the browser where to get it.

type tells the browser what format the video has been produced in.

" *The tablet device is going to be the dominant form of entertainment for kids over the next few years.*

Michael Acton-Smith, creator of Moshi Monsters **"**

✳ MULTIMEDIA

Multimedia is term used to describe a mix of different types of media such as images, text, film and music.

When designing your app you might like to think about how you can use multimedia to make your pages more interesting and to get your message across. For example, you might find a particular funny film on YouTube featuring an animal which you could put on your page so everyone else can see the animal in action.

Remember though, unless you've made it yourself, you will need to be careful to ensure that you have permission to use any material you include.

✳ ADDING LINKS

Navigation between two pages and in our hybrid app is all about **hyperlinks**. You may know hyperlinks as the things you click on to jump from one website to another, but you can also use links to move people between pages in your app, to explore functionality on a phone or even to send people to websites you like on the Internet (these would launch in a smartphone's browser).

We've seen how to build single page, but to create the user journey we looked at earlier in the book (page 19) you will need to make some more pages and add some links to connect them together.

There are two things you need to create a link:

✳ the name of a file you want to link to

✳ the link **hotspot**, the highlighted text or graphic that you click on to get to where you want to go.

To create a link in HTML 5, you will need the **anchor (or link) tag <a>**. This is a container tag so you know it will wrap around the text or image you want to make into a link like this:

<a>...</a>

Inside the tag, you need a file name attribute to tell the browser where to go. So the **basic code for a link looks like this:**

a – this stands for 'anchor' and that tells the browser this is a link

href – the hypertext reference tells the browser where to go on the Internet

```
<a href="cutequestion.html">
Start searching for a pet</a>
```

url – this is the destination of the link

text – this is the text that will be linked to the destination of the web page

✳ USEFUL HTML 5 TAGS

The trick to mastering HTML 5 is to learn the tags and have a go to see what they do. To get you started, here is a list of some of the most commonly used HTML 5 tags.

Tag	Description
`<a>`	Anchor or link
`<audio>`	Inserts an audio file
`<body>`	Document body
` `	Single line break
`<caption>`	Table caption
`<em>`	Defines emphasized text
`<footer>`	Information at the bottom of the page
`<header>`	Information about a page
`<html>`	HTML document
`<i>`	Italics
`<img>`	Image
`<li>`	List item
`<mark>`	Highlight
`<nav>`	Shows a navigation element
`<ol>`	Ordered list
`<p>`	Paragraph
`<strong>`	Bold text with semantic emphasis
`<style>`	Style information for a page
`<table>`	Table
`<tbody>`	Body content in a table
`<title>`	Title for a page
`<ul>`	Unordered list
`<video>`	Inserts a video file

There are too many HTML 5 tags to list them all here but you can find a great quick reference list for all of them at www.htmlgoodies.com.

DIY DUDE

Make a new page

To make another page quickly, run through the page creation process we have already covered. Don't forget that you'll need some different text and images on your new page and you'll need to call it something unique. When you name your new page you should follow some simple rules:

* Don't leave spaces in the file name.

* Always end with '.html' to tell a browser that this is an HTML page.

* Don't use funny symbols like: $, %, ^, &.

Choose the 'Save as' option on the File menu and name your page, for example 'photos.html'.

Now return to your original page and type in your link code but reference your new page as part of the resource location in the URL. So

<a href="http://www.petguru.co.uk/photos.html">Follow this link to start choosing your pet</a>

Save the page and refresh your browser. You should now see your highlighted link. Click it and the browser will take you to your new page.

Congratulations! You've just made your first link and your first HTML 5 website at the same time!

Dude!

QUICK EXPERT SUMMARY

- HTML 5 tags tell browsers how to display content.

- HTML 5 is built from a library of tags.

- HTML 5 contains semantic elements and you can easily insert video and audio.

- Be careful about the copyright of images used online.

- Nest your tags to make it easy to read your code.

MAKING IT **LOOK GOOD**

✳ USING CSS

So we have seen how HTML 5 can be used to define the words, images and links on a web page, but you will still need to tell the browser how you would like your pages and ultimately your app to look. This is your chance to add loads of creativity and colour to help make your pages stand out.

We do this by using CSS (Cascading Style Sheets) a style sheet language used to define the presentation of pages written in a mark-up language (such as HTML). CSS allows you to add information to a page that can be read by your browser about how each page is displayed. For example the background of your page, the colour of any links and what font the text should be displayed in.

You can do this in one of two ways:

✳ You can put a separate style sheet on each page

Or

✳ You can create one style sheet and link all your pages to it

We only have so much time in this book, so we will just look at adding some styling to an individual page. However there are loads of great styling resources online and we'd recommend a visit to CSS Zen Garden at www.ccszengarden.com to see some fantastic examples of what styling your page can do.

REALITY CHECK

 Ethan Duggan

Ethan Duggan is an 11-year-old schoolboy in Las Vegas who found himself running out of encouraging comments when his mum asked him about new clothes she had bought. Following a shopping trip from which his mum returned with 'about 40 dresses, skirts, and tops' Ethan decided to act.

He taught himself to code on Codeacademy during his summer holidays picking up HTML, CSS and JavaScript and – using PhoneGap – published the LazyHusband app on the Android, iPhone and Windows platforms.

LazyHusband compiled a series of key phrases that can be played back over a smartphone to order, such as "you look great", "you're beautiful" and "wow".

Ethan has since followed up the app with LazyWife and LazyKid apps and was invited to speak at a major coding conference in Texas. It's unclear if his mother was as enthusiastic about his work as the developer community.

OFFICIAL FORM C-185A

✳ WRITING A STYLE SHEET

Style sheets may seem tricky when you first look at them but they are similar to HTML 5 because they use attributes to tell the browser what to do. CSS syntax consists of only 3 parts and they are always written like this:

selector { property: value }

Don't worry, this is easier than it looks. Here's what that means:

selector — Is the HTML element that you want to style (such as a heading tag).

Property — Is what style it will create (e.g. changing the colour of something).

value — Defines how the style is applied (such as in the colour red).

You will need to remember that HTML attributes are usually framed by angle brackets like this: <attribute> whereas style sheets hold their attributes with curly brackets (they really are called that!) or braces like this: {attribute}.

✳ ADDING A STYLE SHEET TO YOUR PAGE

Let's see how this might work if we add a style sheet into our page. To do this you will need to follow a couple of rules:

❂ It must be within the <head> and </head> commands.

❂ The text must be surrounded by <style type="text/css"> and </style>

When you're all done, the format will look like this:

```
<head>
<style type="text/css">
```

Style Sheet information goes in here...

```
</style>
</head>
```

Let's look at an actual example of CSS in action:

```
<html>
<head>
<style type="text/css">

body
{
background-color:#d0e4fe;
}
h1
{
color:red;
text-align:center;
font-family:"verdana";
}
p
{
font-family:"arial";
font-size:20px;
}
</style>
<title>My top-twenty hamster breeds</title>
</head>
```

background-color – tells the browser what colour to make the page. (Don't worry, spelling is deliberate! HTML uses American spellings.)

h1 – tells the browser which font and colour to use for the heading.

p – tells the browser which font and colour to use for the text within paragraph tags.

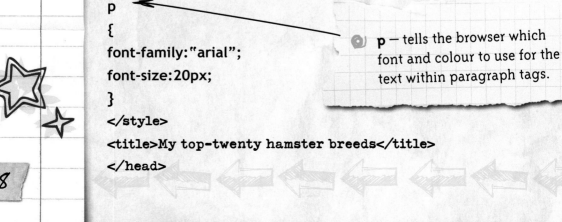

DEFINING COLOURING AND SIZE

Colour and text size can be defined in two ways in style sheets — one's easy and the other's a bit trickier.

A colour can be defined by its name, such as orange, or by a more precise hexadecimal definition. A hexadecimal colour is a six-digit number used to represent the red, green and blue components of that colour. The first two digits are red, the second two digits are green and the third two are blue. The colours run from 0 to 6, then from A to F. Numbers mean low and letters mean high amounts of that colour. So the 'hex colour' for white is #ffffff and the 'hex colour' for black is #000000.

Likewise size can be defined by a simple number from 1 to 5, with 1 being the largest, or by a more precise definition in points, an old printing term. For example the text in this paragraph is in 12pt.

ADDING A BUTTON

To add a button you will need to tell the browser about a section of CSS devoted solely to button-styling known as a class. There's one below. It should all look pretty familiar, but you will notice that we have named the class by adding '#button' before the first curly bracket.

```
#button {
    width: 100px;
    height: 30px;
    background-color: purple;
    font-size: 12pt;
    font-family: Verdana;
    font-weight: bold;
    text-align: center;}
```

To add a class simply insert it between the <style> tags in the document head.

You can tell the browser where to apply the style by wrapping your hyperlink in another container tag know as a <span> tag. Span tags are simply blank tags that carry information. The information it will carry here is the ID for the class. So...

```
<span id="button"><a href="cutequestion.html">Start
searching for a pet</a></span>
```

DIY DUDE

Add some
CSS styling

I guess you can imagine what's coming next...
That's right – you're going to add some styling to your page. Open your document in your text editor and type in the code on page 48 between the <head> tags. You can change the colours and fonts to whatever you like. When you are done, save the file and reload the page.

How's that page looking?
Colourful, right?
That's exactly what we want.

Dude!

SOME DESIGN DOS AND DON'TS

To help make your app as professional as possible, here are some tips that might help as you decide on the look of your pages....

- ◉ DO try using some images of your own to make your page unique.

- ◉ DON'T be afraid to leave some space on your page. A cluttered app is hard to read.

- ◉ DO use a larger font for titles (h1 or h2).

- ◉ DON'T use fonts and colour schemes that are difficult to look at, so DON'T use dark fonts on a dark background or bright, neon colours.

- ◉ DO choose a colour scheme and design that suits you and the theme of your app.

- ◉ DON'T use too many large images as they can slow the time it takes to load a page.

- ◉ DO use buttons rather than links for easy finger clicking.

- ◉ DON'T let your pages go on too long — no one likes to scroll.

- ◉ DO keep your navigation in one place (like the top the page).

Remember it's your app and you're choosing the content and how to present it — so don't be afraid to be creative!

QUICK EXPERT SUMMARY

- ◉ Style sheets define the look and feel of a page.
- ◉ Both HTML 5 and style sheets have a standard syntax.
- ◉ Keep your design uncluttered and easy to read.

GETTING YOUR
APP ONLINE

✳ WHERE DO APPS LIVE?

All apps need to live somewhere but where? The short answer is that ultimately your app will live on someone's smartphone, tablet or mobile device when someone downloads it but it will have to go on a bit of a journey to get there.

Apps, like websites, are collections of code that are held on a computer until someone wants to access them — this is called **hosting**. An app's host is a dedicated computer known as a **server** that sits in a building somewhere in the world. This is where your app is kept when you put it on the App Store or Play Store because they are both simply big servers (or groups of servers) hosting thousands of apps.

As the Internet is a global network of computers that are all connected to each other, it doesn't matter where you live or where the server hosting your app is located — you could be in Edinburgh but your app could be hosted in Los Angeles, Madrid, Tokyo or even in the middle of the Antarctic!

Our hybrid app is going to be hosted in multiple places — the App and Play Stores and a web host if you want to have your HTML 5 online as a website. The good news is that this means there are loads of places for people to find out about the app and start using it.

If you choose to have your app online as a website, the hosting is something you might have to pay for. Choosing a web hosting provider is easy. There's a huge number of web hosts out there and most offer a similar service for a small charge. Try to do your research with someone who has done it before and look for free options closer to home before you fork out your own cash — for example your school might have some space you could borrow.

You don't need to buy any hosting to use this Quick Expert's Guide and you can build and browse the HTML 5 website that will underpin your app without it. When that's done then you can decide whether you want to put it online.

>> THE BOFFIN BIT <<

IN APP

In App is the name given to a purchase made or service delivered within an application installed on a mobile device. An example of this might be purchasing extra weapons in a game or additional lessons in a learning app. Such purchases are usually made via the App Store, and online payment systems such as PayPal.

Delivering additional or collectable content is a great way for app developers to make money when their apps have been given away free or sold at a low price. It is good for users too, as they have had a chance to try the product and decide if they like it before handing over their cash.

In app purchasing is part of a growing 'virtual economy' of goods and service online. Don't worry – people are making real money from these sales – this economy is only described as virtual because the products are lines of code rather than real things (such as items of food or clothing).

✳ TIME TO PACKAGE UP YOUR APP

The program we are going to use to get your app online is an opensource product from Adobe called PhoneGap Build. You can find it at https://build.phonegap.com. PhoneGap Build will host your app locally so you can share it privately with a small group of friends to test your app. When you are ready it can also compile your code for any mobile operating system. It sounds like a lot of work for nothing and Adobe will charge for heavy or business users of the system but a basic account is all free. Nice!

Zipping up your app

Before you start you will need to get all your code in one place. A **zip file** is a way of collecting pages, pictures and code into a single file and compressing them so they can be easily transferred between computers. To create a zip file, simply make a new folder on your desktop and copy all the files for your app into it. Then right click on the file to show the action menu and select 'Send to' and 'Compressed folder' if you use a PC or 'Compress' if you use a Mac. Either one of these options will now create another file on your desktop, it will be called the same as your original file but probably have a zip on it. It's pretty obvious but... that's your zip file.

Starting with PhoneGap Build

To upload anything to PhoneGap you will need to create an account. After hitting the Get Started button, you will see that there are two ways to do this. Probably the easiest is to sign up for an Adobe account. This is free and you will just need an email address to do so. After that, you are ready to go. The next thing you will see is that PhoneGap will ask you to upload a zip file of your code. Luckily we've already got one so...

Making your apps

Select the 'Upload a .zip file' button to send across your zip file. You can use the file navigation tree that pops up on your screen to find it on your computer. Hit open and that's it. You will see that PhoneGap immediately goes to work building all the files you need be they Android, iOS, Blackberry, Windows, whatever... The next page will give you a selection of files to download for various operating systems — they will all be different file types from .apk to .xap but all you need to worry about is uploading the right file for the right operating system when the time comes.

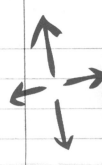

>> THE BOFFIN BIT <<

SERVERS

A **server** is the name given to a powerful computer that hosts websites, databases and email systems and makes them available over the Internet.

A server functions much like your desktop computer but it has a faster processor to give it more power as well as more memory and multiple hard drives to help it complete lots of tasks at the same time. Servers may also run their own kind of operating systems that are designed for heavy usage, such as UNIX, Linux or Windows Server.

✳ CREATING A DEVELOPER ACCOUNT

Both the Android Play Store and Apple App Store will require you to register for a developer account in order to upload an app. For the Play Store this is free but you will have to pay Apple to open a developer account on the App Store. You will need to ask someone with a credit card to pay for this.

When you register as a developer you will be given a **public key** — this is your private ID linked to your profile (known as a **certificate**). Keep it safe as you will need to give it to PhoneGap every time you create an app.

>> THE BOFFIN BIT <<

TESTING APPS

Testing mobile apps is really tricky and everyone from professional developers to people coding for fun faces the same issues. There are three key reasons why:

1. There is a huge variety of mobile handsets so your app must work with dozens of different screen sizes and keyboards.

2. There are different operating systems from Android to Symbian and that means that only correctly coded apps will be supported by them.

3. Different mobile operators around the world use their own network standards (such as CDMA or GSM) to deliver data in different ways. This means that there are loads of issues with code, especially how different devices handle scripting languages.

There are some expensive pieces of software that can be bought – and some free ones – that will automatically test your app across multiple handsets. However many developers resort to checking their work by hand on as many different smartphones as they can get hold of.

For our purpose, we suggest you focus on the phone and operating system most popular with your friends and build for that. If most of your friends have HTC phones and Android operating systems, make sure your app works for them and worry about the rest later.

✳ SUBMITTING AN APP

We're nearly there... When you upload a file from PhoneGap Build to the App Store or Play Store you will need to give them a little bit of information about your app. Each site will ask you slightly different questions but it's worth having a think about the following:

✳ **Where it should sit?** What category should it be indexed under, for example games.

✳ **How would you rate your content?** Is it for everyone at any age or just for older people?

✳ **Which part of the world should use it?** Is for people in the UK or the whole world?

✳ **Does it cost to download your app?** Is it free or paid for?

You will also need to submit a description of what your app does, a link to your website if you have one and any promotional images such as a logo or screenshots. Luckily, we produced an excellent logo when we thought about badging our app — so don't forget to use that.

✳ HOW WILL SOMEONE FIND MY APP?

If you added up all the world's Android, Apple and Blackberry apps there would probably be over 2 million. So how will anyone find yours?

Luckily both the App Store and Play Store have pretty whizzy search engines, so people can find your app by name if they know it. Also all the information you uploaded with your app will help them to place your app in a category where people might find it.

Even better, both Google and Apple make the listings on their stores available on the Internet as web pages so there is a chance that anyone doing a web search might also be able to find your app. This is all the more reason to make sure that the logos, name, description and screenshot you supply with your app are as good as possible.

Reviews and recommendations

Ultimately what will increase your profile on the App and Play Stores is people downloading your app, so tell your friends and family about it. They can help more people to download the app by reviewing and rating your work positively. A good word from another person can make all the difference to someone deciding whether or not to download your app so make sure you ask them to leave an upbeat review and give it a five star rating!

SAY WHAT?

" *The secret is that you have to be a bit crazy. We want to change the world, and you have to be a bit crazy to believe that you can. A lot of people thought we were crazy when we said we wanted to get 100 million downloads, but we now have 700 million...* **"**

Peter Vesterbacka, creator of Angry Birds, on inspiration for apps.

QUICK EXPERT SUMMARY

- ⊚ Apps are hosted on the App or Play Stores until they are downloaded to a smartphone.

- ⊚ Zip up your files to pass them between computers.

- ⊚ PhoneGap will create different file types for different operating systems.

- ⊚ You will need a developer account to upload an app.

- ⊚ Make sure friends and family rate and review your work.

THE LAST WORD ON CREATING AN APP

Having **dipped your toe** in the water of HTML 5 programming, hopefully you can now **go forth** and create your own **amazing app.** The most important thing to remember is **to have fun!**

Useful links

Coding

HTML Goodies — A great resource of online tutorials on all things web. www.htmlgoodies.com

W3 schools — The definitive directory of web standards http://www.w3schools.com/html/html5_intro.asp

W3C — The definitive directory of web standards. www.w3c.org

Github — Free online repository to store and share your code. github.com/

Design and CSS

CSS ZEN Garden — Great examples of the power of CSS. www.csszengarden.com

W3schools CSS — Everything you need to know about style sheets www.w3schools.com/css/

W3schools HTML colours — A chart of HTML colours http://w3schools.com/html/html_colors.asp

GIMP: GNU Image Manipulation Program — Opensource image manipulation software. www.gimp.org

Free images

Creative Commons — A searchable database of reusable content and images search.creativecommons.org/

Morguefile — A collection of free images of all kinds. www.morguefile.com

App building

Adobe PhoneGAP — A handy opensource tool to create mobile apps of all kinds. build.phonegap.com

Appshed — A website that will allow you to build and design apps online using a drag and drop interface. www.appshed.com

Mobile testing tools

Mobile Me — A website that will allow you to test your designs on different phones and devices. http://mobiletest.me/

Learning to code

Apps for Good — A school based programme training people to produce apps for social good. http://www.appsforgood.org

Freeformers — Accessible hack days for young people and a network of weekly tech jams to meet others and hone your skills http://www.freeformers.com

Coder Dojo — Learn code at a local code club near to you. http://coderdojo.com

Code Academy — Learn to code online and share the results with your friends. http://www.codecademy.com/

accelerometer — a device that senses movement in a smartphone.

Android — the operating system used by Android devices.

app — a self-contained software application that runs on a mobile device or computer.

App Store — online distribution network for apps used by Apple devices.

attribute — Additional information describing the use of a tag or style element.

browser — a program that is used to view web pages.

container tag — an HTML tag used in an opening and closing pair and wrapped around content.

CSS — Cascading Style Sheets

empty tag — an HTML tag that stands alone.

GIF — Graphic Interchange Format

Github — a shared online repository of code used by developers.

GPS — Global Positioning System

gyroscope — a device that senses orientation in a smartphone.

hexadecimal colour — a numerical representation of colour used in HTML.

HTML — Hypertext MarkUp Language

hybrid apps — HTML 5 websites that are designed to run as apps.

hypertext — the name given to content created in HTML.

Internet — a global network of connected computers.

iOS — the operating system used by Apple devices.

JPEG — Joint Photographic Experts Group

mobile OS — the underlying operating system of a smartphone.

multimedia — images, video, sounds and text combined on the web.

native apps — bespoke apps built to work with the operating system of a smartphone.

opensource — Free software developed and maintained online.

paper prototype — a way of visualizing app design using paper.

pixels — the basic units that make up an image displayed on a computer screen.

Play Store — online distribution network for apps used by Android devices.

PNG — Portable Network Graphic

private key — your personal developer ID, usually attached to a certificate.

semantic mark-up — HTML 5 tags used to indicate the layout of a web page.

server — a computer connected to the Internet that hosts and serves websites.

smartphone — an Internet-enabled mobile phone that can perform many of the functions of a computer.

SMS — Short Message Service (another name for texts)

style sheet — a text document that gives a browser information about the design of a website.

tablet — a mobile computer usually with screen, keyboard and processor all in one unit.

tag — a piece of code that gives direction to a browser in HTML.

touchscreen — a visual interface to entering data to a smartphone.

usability — the study of user interaction with websites.

user journey — the path taken through an app or website.

WC3 — World Wide Web Consortium

web page — a text file written in HTML.

website — A collection of web pages held under one URL.